# Blake Griffin

**by Josh Gregory**

Consultant: Charlie Zegers
Sports Journalist

BEARPORT
PUBLISHING

New York, New York

**Credits**

Cover and Title Page, © Damian Dovarganes/AP Images, © Robbins Photography, and © Shea Walsh/AP Images; 4, © Mark J. Terrill/AP Images; 5, © Mark J. Terrill/AP Images; 6, © Sue Ogrocki/AP Images; 7, © Sue Ogrocki/AP Images; 9, © Ed Reinke/AP Images; 10, © Robbins Photography; 11, © Robbins Photography; 12, © Robbins Photography; 13, © Seth Wenig/AP Images; 14, © Jae C. Hon/AP Images; 15, © Robbins Photography; 16, © Danny Moloshok; 17, © Shea Walsh/AP Images; 18, © AP Images; 19, © Mark J. Terrill/AP Images; 20, © Minerva Studio/Shutterstock; 21, © Robbins Photography; 22L, © Staff/MCT/Newscom; 22R, © Robbins Photography.

Publisher: Kenn Goin
Editor: Jessica Rudolph
Creative Director: Spencer Brinker
Photo Researcher: Josh Gregory

*Library of Congress Cataloging-in-Publication Data*

Gregory, Josh.
  Blake Griffin / by Josh Gregory.
      pages cm. — (Basketball heroes making a difference)
  Includes bibliographical references and index.
  ISBN 978-1-62724-081-9 (library binding) — ISBN 1-62724-081-0 (library binding)
  1.  Griffin, Blake, 1989—-Juvenile literature. 2.  Basketball players—United States—Biography—
Juvenile literature.  I. Title.
  GV884.G76G74 2014
  796.323092—dc23
  [B]
                                          2013037785

For more information, write to Bearport Publishing Company, Inc., 45 West 21st Street, Suite 3B, New York, New York 10010. Printed in the United States of America.

10 9 8 7 6 5 4 3 2 1

# Contents

# A Slam-Dunk Start

On October 27, 2010, basketball fans at the Staples Center in Los Angeles, California, were on the edge of their seats. **Rookie** Blake Griffin charged down the court alongside his Los Angeles Clippers teammates. The Clippers were playing the Portland Trail Blazers. It was the first **NBA** game for the young **forward**.

As Blake raced to the basket, he saw that his teammate Randy Foye had the ball. Randy dribbled the ball once, then tossed it to Blake. Blake jumped into the air, grabbed the ball, and slam-dunked it. The crowd went wild! Blake had just scored his first points in the NBA.

Blake (left) celebrates a basket with teammate Randy Foye during the game against the Trail Blazers.

Blake dunks during his first NBA game, against the Portland Trail Blazers.

Blake scored 20 points and pulled down 14 **rebounds** in his first NBA game.

# Little Griffin

People who knew Blake weren't surprised by his success in his first NBA game. Blake has been surrounded by basketball his whole life.

When Blake was growing up, his father, Tommy, coached basketball at a high school in Oklahoma. Tommy encouraged Blake and his older brother, Taylor, to play the game. The two boys practiced in their driveway. Blake was younger and smaller than Taylor, but he competed fiercely to beat his brother. For many years, Blake and Taylor played sports in youth leagues. The brothers soon became two of the best young basketball players in Oklahoma.

Taylor (far left) and Blake (second from left) have a close relationship with their parents, Tommy and Gail (right).

Blake (front) and Taylor
(back, in white) playing
together in a college
basketball game

Blake Austin Griffin was born
in Oklahoma City, Oklahoma,
on March 16, 1989.

# A Basketball Family

In 2003, both Griffin boys enrolled at Oklahoma Christian School. Together, they joined the high school's basketball team, which their father coached. During Blake's freshman season, the Oklahoma Christian Saints didn't lose a single game. The team won the state championship in both his freshman and sophomore years.

During those two seasons, Taylor was the biggest star on the team. Then Taylor graduated and headed off to college at the University of Oklahoma. Now it was Blake's turn in the spotlight. By his junior year, Blake had grown very tall. He could jump high and crowd out other players to pull down rebounds. He was also very fast and a terrific shooter. In his junior and senior years, Blake led the team to two more state championships.

During high school, an Oklahoma newspaper named Blake Player of the Year two years in a row.

In 2007, Blake played in the McDonald's All-American Game. The best high school basketball players in the country compete in this game every year.

# Soaring with the Sooners

Many colleges tried to **recruit** Blake to join their basketball teams. After high school, Blake decided to stay close to home and join his brother at the University of Oklahoma. Taylor was already a star on the college's basketball team, the Sooners. However, in no time Blake became one of the top ten scorers and rebounders in the team's **conference**.

Basketball fans around the nation were astonished by Blake's powerful dunks. His great performances on the court continued during his sophomore season. That year, Blake racked up 30 **double-doubles** and pulled down more rebounds than any college player in the previous 30 years!

Blake (right) plays for the Sooners in a 2009 game against the University of Missouri Tigers.

Blake was so good during his freshman year at the University of Oklahoma that many fans expected him to leave college early to join the NBA.

Blake was chosen as his conference's Player of the Year during his sophomore season at the University of Oklahoma.

# A Rough Start

At the end of his sophomore basketball season, Blake was ready to become a pro player. In 2009, he left college and entered the NBA **draft**. That year, the Los Angeles Clippers chose him as the first overall pick!

Blake was thrilled to be in the big leagues. He began training with the Clippers, and he played well during the **preseason games**. However, Blake did not get a chance to shine in the regular season. In the Clippers' last preseason game, Blake broke his kneecap while landing during one of his famous dunks. Blake was crushed when his doctors told him that he would have to miss the entire season because of his injury. Would his pro basketball career be over before it even began?

Blake (center), shown here during a 2013 game, quickly fit in with his teammates after joining the Clippers in 2009.

Blake shakes hands with NBA Commissioner David Stern at the 2009 NBA draft.

At six feet ten inches (2.08 m), Blake stands taller than most NBA players.

# Reaching New Heights

Blake didn't let his injury hold him back. After having surgery on his knee, he trained hard to get back in shape. Yet he worried about playing in the 2010–2011 season. Blake had sat on the sidelines for an entire year. Could he still make it in the NBA?

Blake quickly put those fears to rest. That season, he led the team in rebounds and points per game. However, the Clippers did not make the **playoffs**. The next season, the team added star player Chris Paul to the team. Chris and Blake were incredible partners on the court. As a result, the team made it all the way to the second round of the playoffs. With Blake leading the way, the Clippers were becoming one of the NBA's best teams.

Blake (left) with Chris Paul (right) during a 2013 game

Because Blake
missed all of the
regular season games
of 2009–2010, his
rookie year was the
2010–2011 season.

Blake was chosen as the NBA Rookie
of the Year in the 2010–2011 season.

# Dunking for Dollars

Many people look up to Blake as a role model. One way he tries to set a good example is by **promoting** healthy habits. Blake knows that staying active helps keep people healthy. "I think it's just important to be active as a kid," he has said. "Growing up, that's all my brother and I did."

During his rookie season in 2010–2011, Blake started encouraging kids to eat right and exercise. He decided that every time he made a slam dunk in a game, he would give $100 to **charity**. The money would go to help fight childhood **obesity**. That season, Blake made 214 slam dunks!

As one of the NBA's top dunkers, Blake knew that his pledge to donate money for each dunk he made would add up quickly.

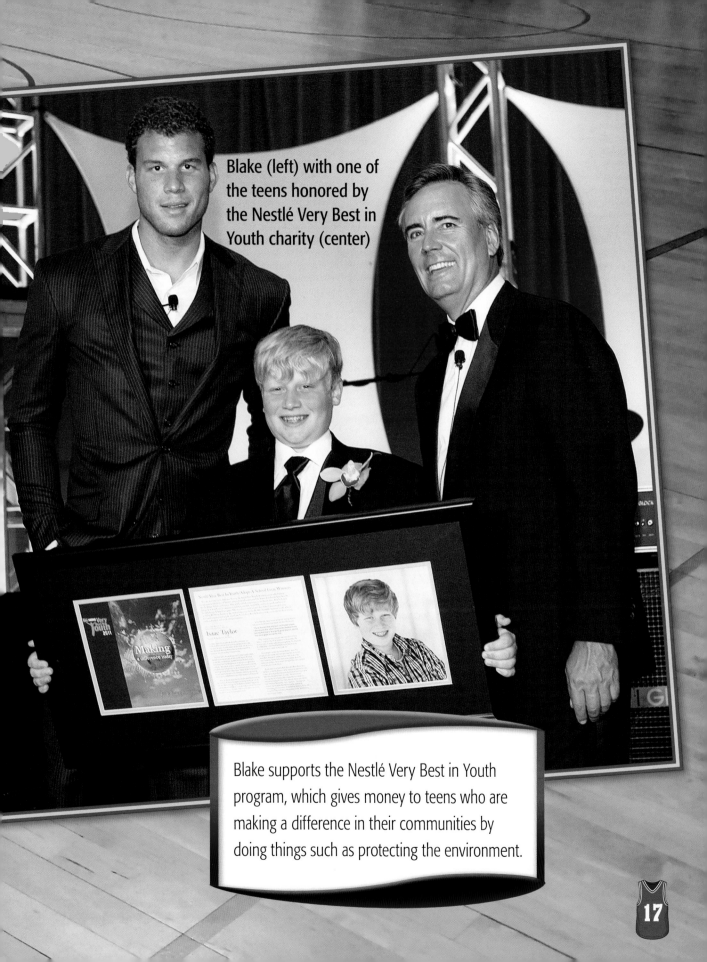

Blake (left) with one of the teens honored by the Nestlé Very Best in Youth charity (center)

Blake supports the Nestlé Very Best in Youth program, which gives money to teens who are making a difference in their communities by doing things such as protecting the environment.

# Standing Up to Cancer

Another cause that is important to Blake is finding a cure for cancer. In 2011, Blake's high school basketball teammate Wilson Holloway died from the disease. Wilson passed away just a few days before the annual NBA Slam Dunk Contest.

Losing his close friend encouraged Blake to do everything he could to help fight cancer. That year, Blake won the dunk competition by jumping over the top of a car and slamming the ball into the basket. Afterward, he autographed the car and **auctioned** it off for charity. The money was given to an organization called Stand Up To Cancer. Blake was happy he could honor the memory of his friend Wilson by raising **funds** for cancer research.

Blake with teammate Baron Davis at the 2011 dunk contest

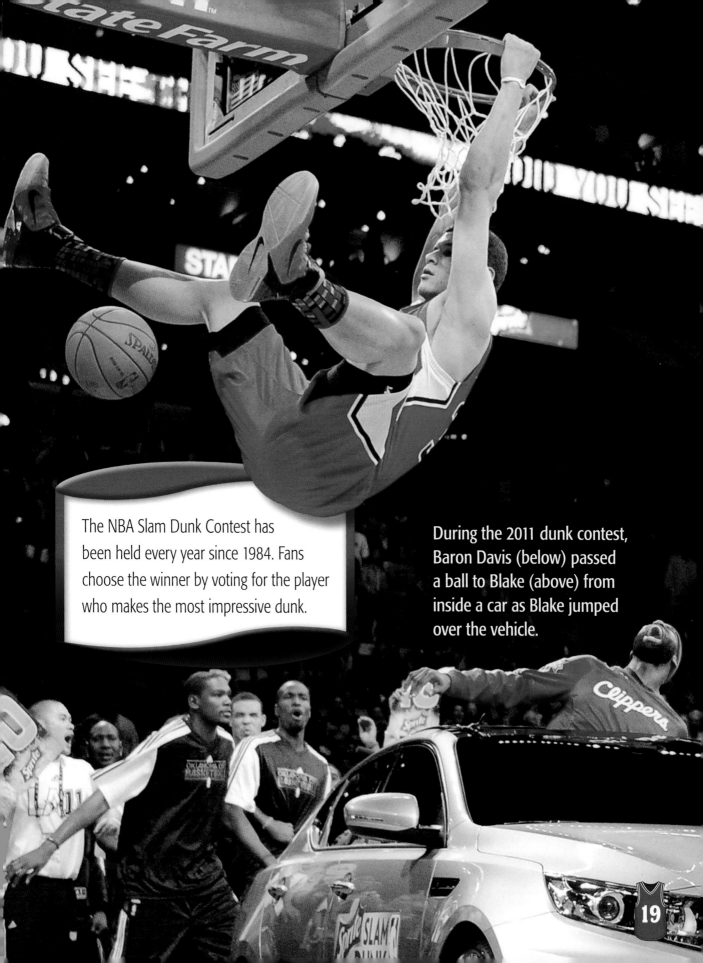

The NBA Slam Dunk Contest has been held every year since 1984. Fans choose the winner by voting for the player who makes the most impressive dunk.

During the 2011 dunk contest, Baron Davis (below) passed a ball to Blake (above) from inside a car as Blake jumped over the vehicle.

# Relief and Rebuilding

Today, Blake continues to do big things on the court. In the 2012–2013 NBA season, he led the Clippers to their first **division** championship. With Blake's help, the Clippers are better than ever. Fans hope Blake and his teammates can go even farther in the coming seasons.

In the meantime, Blake still works to help people in need. In 2013, he and his brother started the Griffin Family Relief Fund. The charity raises money for victims of a deadly tornado that hit the town of Moore, Oklahoma, in May 2013. Moore is located near the Griffins' hometown of Oklahoma City. While Blake's incredible dunks are what made him famous, it is his work helping others that makes him a true hero.

The Moore tornado killed 23 people and caused around $2 billion worth of damage.

After winning their first division championship in 2013, Blake and the Clippers played the Memphis Grizzlies in the NBA Western Conference Semifinals.

# The Blake File

Blake is a basketball hero on and off the court. Here are some highlights.

LOS ANGELES CLIPPERS

- Blake and Taylor Griffin were both drafted by NBA teams in the same season. Blake was the first overall pick, while Taylor was 48th.

- During Blake's rookie season, he was ranked the tenth-best player in the entire NBA by the television sports network ESPN.

- One of Blake's best friends when he was growing up was Sam Bradford, who is now a pro football player for the St. Louis Rams.

- Blake has played in the NBA All-Star Game in every season of his professional career. The All-Star Game is a special game held each season that features two teams made up of the NBA's best players.

- Blake was chosen to play basketball for the U.S. Olympic team in 2012. He couldn't play, however, because he was recovering from a knee injury.

# Glossary

**auctioned** (AWK-shuhnd) sold to a buyer who offered the most money

**charity** (CHA-ruh-tee) a group that tries to help people in need

**conference** (KAHN-fur-uhnss) a group of sports teams that compete mainly with one another

**division** (dih-VIZH-uhn) a group of teams within a conference

**double-doubles** (DUH-buhl-DUH-buhlz) having a double-digit statistic in two categories, such as points and rebounds, during one game

**draft** (DRAFT) an event in which professional teams take turns choosing new athletes to play for them

**forward** (FOR-wurd) one of the standard positions on a basketball team that is often responsible for much of the team's scoring; a team's two forwards are generally taller than the guards but shorter than the team's center

**funds** (FUHNDS) money collected to be used for a specific purpose

**NBA** (EHN-BEE-AY) letters standing for the National Basketball Association, the professional men's basketball league in North America

**obesity** (oh-BEESS-uh-tee) a condition where a person is extremely overweight

**playoffs** (PLAY-awfss) a series of games that determine which teams will play in a championship

**preseason games** (PREE-see-zuhn GAYMZ) a series of games that take place before the regular season starts

**promoting** (pruh-MOHT-ing) making the public aware of something

**rebounds** (REE-boundz) balls that are caught by players after missed shots

**recruit** (ri-KROOT) to persuade an athlete to attend a college and play for its sports teams

**rookie** (RUK-ee) a first-year player

23